THOMAS À KEMPIS

COUNSELS ON THE SPIRITUAL LIFE

TRANSLATED BY LEO SHERLEY-PRICE

PENGUIN BOOKS

PENGUIN BOOKS

Published by the Penguin Group
Penguin Books Ltd, 27 Wrights Lane, London w8 5tz, England
Penguin Books USA Inc., 375 Hudson Street, New York, New York 10014, USA
Penguin Books Australia Ltd, Ringwood, Victoria, Australia
Penguin Books Canada Ltd, 10 Alcorn Avenue, Toronto, Ontario, Canada m4v 3b2
Penguin Books (NZ) Ltd, 182–190 Wairau Road, Auckland 10, New Zealand

Penguin Books Ltd, Registered Offices: Harmondsworth, Middlesex, England

These extracts are from *The Imitation of Christ*, by Thomas à Kempis, translated
by Leo Sherley-Price, first published in Penguin Classics 1952
This edition published 1995
1 3 5 7 9 10 8 6 4 2

Typeset by Rowland Phototypesetting Ltd, Bury St Edmunds, Suffolk
Printed in England by Clays Ltd, St Ives plc

CONTENTS

On the Imitation of Christ

'He who follows Me shall not walk in darkness,' says Our Lord.[1]

In these words Christ counsels us to follow His life and way if we desire true enlightenment and freedom from all blindness of heart.[2] Let the life of Jesus Christ, then, be our first consideration.

The teaching of Jesus far transcends all the teachings of the Saints, and whosoever has His spirit will discover concealed in it heavenly manna.[3] But many people, although they often hear the Gospel, feel little desire to follow it, because they lack the spirit of Christ.[4] Whoever desires to understand and take delight in the words of Christ must strive to conform his whole life to Him.

1. John 8:12. 2. Mark 3:5. 3. Rev. 2:17.
4. Rom. 8:9.

Of what use is it to discourse learnedly on the Trinity, if you lack humility and therefore displease the Trinity? Lofty words do not make a man just or holy; but a good life makes him dear to God. I would far rather feel contrition than be able to define it. If you knew the whole Bible by heart, and all the teachings of the philosophers, how would this help you without the grace and love of God? 'Vanity of vanities, and all is vanity,'[5] except to love God and serve Him alone.[6] And this is supreme wisdom – to despise the world, and draw daily nearer the kingdom of heaven.

It is vanity to solicit honours, or to raise oneself to high station. It is vanity to be a slave to bodily desires,[7] and to crave for things which bring certain retribution. It is vanity to wish for long life, if you care little for a good life. It is vanity to give thought only to this present life, and to care nothing for the life to come. It is vanity to love things that so swiftly pass

5. Eccles. 1:2.   6. Deut. 6:13.   7. Gal. 5:16.

away, and not to hasten onwards to that place where everlasting joy abides.

Keep constantly in mind the saying, 'The eye is not satisfied with seeing, nor the ear filled with hearing.'[8] Strive to withdraw your heart from the love of visible things, and direct your affections to things invisible. For those who follow only their natural inclinations defile their conscience, and lose the grace of God.

8. Eccles. 1:8.

2
On Personal Humility

Everyone naturally desires knowledge,[1] but of what use is knowledge itself without the fear of God? A humble countryman who serves God is more pleasing to Him than a conceited intellectual who knows the course of the stars, but neglects his own soul.[2] A man who truly knows himself realizes his own worthlessness, and takes no pleasure in the praises of men. Did I possess all knowledge in the world, but had no love,[3] how would this help me before God, who will judge me by my deeds?

Restrain an inordinate desire for knowledge, in which is found much anxiety and deception. Learned men always wish to appear so, and desire recognition of their wisdom. But there are many matters, knowledge of which brings

1. Aristotle, *Metaphysics*, I, 1.
2. Ecclus. 19.22.   3. 1 Cor. 13:2.

little or no advantage to the soul. Indeed, a man is unwise if he occupies himself with any things save those that further his salvation. A spate of words does nothing to satisfy the soul, but a good life refreshes the mind, and a clean conscience[4] brings great confidence in God.

The more complete and excellent your knowledge, the more severe will be God's judgement on you, unless your life be the more holy. Therefore, do not be conceited of any skill or knowledge you may possess, but respect the knowledge that is entrusted to you. If it seems to you that you know a great deal and have wide experience in many fields, yet remember that there are many matters of which you are ignorant. So do not be conceited,[5] but confess your ignorance. Why do you wish to esteem yourself above others, when there are many who are wiser and more perfect in the Law of God? If you desire to know or learn anything to your advantage, then take delight in being unknown and unregarded.

4. 1 Tim. 3:9.   5. Rom. 11:20.

5

A true understanding and humble estimate of oneself is the highest and most valuable of all lessons. To take no account of oneself, but always to think well and highly of others, is the highest wisdom and perfection. Should you see another person openly doing evil, or carrying out a wicked purpose, do not on that account consider yourself better than him, for you cannot tell how long you will remain in a state of grace. We are all frail; consider none more frail than yourself.

3
On the Teaching of Truth

Happy the man who is instructed by Truth itself, not by signs and passing words,[1] but as It is in itself. Our own conjectures and observations often mislead us, and we discover little. Of what value are lengthy controversies on deep and obscure matters, when it is not by our knowledge of such things that we shall at length be judged? It is supreme folly to neglect things that are useful and vital, and deliberately turn to curious and harmful things. Truly, 'we have eyes and see not':[2] for what concern to us are such things as *genera* and *species*?

Those to whom the Eternal Word speaks are delivered from uncertainty. From one Word proceed all things,[3] and all things tell of Him; it is He, the Author of all things, who speaks

1. Num. 12:8.   2. Jer. 5:21; John 12:40; Rom. 11:8.
3. John 1:3.

to us.[4] Without Him no one can understand or judge aright. But the man to whom all things are one, who refers everything to One, and who sees everything as in One, is enabled to remain steadfast in heart, and abide at peace with God.

O God, living Truth,[5] unite me to Yourself in everlasting love![6] Often I am wearied by all I read and hear. In You alone is all that I desire and long for. Therefore let all teachers keep silence, and let all creation be still before You; do You, O Lord, speak alone.

The more closely a man is united to You in pure simplicity, the more varied and profound the matters which he understands without effort, for he receives light and understanding from heaven. A pure, simple, and stable man, however busy and occupied, does not become distracted thereby, for he does all things to the glory of God, and strives to preserve himself free from all self-seeking. And what harms and hinders you more than the undisciplined passions of your own heart? A good and devout

4. John 8:25. 5. John 14:6. 6. Jer. 31:3.

8

man firstly sets in order in his mind whatever tasks he has in hand, and never allows them to lead him into occasions of sin, but humbly subjects them to the dictates of a sound judgement. Who has a fiercer struggle than he who strives to conquer himself?[7] Yet this must be our chief concern – to conquer self, and by daily growing stronger than self, to advance in holiness.

All perfection in this life is accompanied by a measure of imperfection, and all our knowledge contains an element of obscurity. A humble knowledge of oneself is a surer road to God than a deep searching of the sciences. Yet learning itself is not to be blamed, nor is the simple knowledge of anything whatsoever to be despised, for true learning is good in itself and ordained by God; but a good conscience and a holy life are always to be preferred. But because many are more eager to acquire much learning than to live well, they often go astray, and bear little or no fruit. If only such people

7. Wisd. 10:12.

were as diligent in the uprooting of vices and the planting of virtues as they are in the debating of problems, there would not be so many evils and scandals among the people, nor such laxity in communities. At the Day of Judgement, we shall not be asked what we have read, but what we have done; not how eloquently we have spoken, but how holily we have lived. Tell me, where are now all those Masters and Doctors whom you knew so well in their lifetime in the full flower of their learning? Other men now sit in their seats, and they are hardly ever called to mind. In their lifetime they seemed of great account, but now no one speaks of them.

Oh, how swiftly the glory of the world passes away![8] If only the lives of these men had been as admirable as their learning, their study and reading would have been to good purpose! But how many in this world care little for the service of God, and perish in their vain learning. Because they choose to be great rather than

8. I John 2:17.

humble, they perish in their own conceit.[9] He is truly great, who is great in the love of God. He is truly great, who is humble in mind, and regards earth's highest honours as nothing. He is truly wise who counts all earthly things as dung, in order that he may win Christ.[10] And he is truly learned, who renounces his own will for the will of God.

---

9. Rom. 1:21.   10. Phil. 3:8.

4
On Prudence in Action

We should not believe every word[1] and sugges-
tion, but should carefully and unhurriedly
consider all things in accordance with the will
of God. For such is the weakness of human
nature, alas, that evil is often more readily
believed and spoken of another than good. But
perfect men do not easily believe every tale that
is told them, for they know that man's nature
is prone to evil,[2] and his words to deception.[3]

It is wise not to be over hasty in action, nor
to cling stubbornly to our own opinions. It is
wise also not to believe all that we hear, nor
to hasten to report to others what we hear or
believe. Take counsel of a wise and conscien-
tious man, and seek[4] to be guided by one who
is better than yourself, rather than to follow

1. Ecclus. 19:16. 2. Gen. 8:21. 3. Ecclus. 14:1.
4. Tobit 4:19.

your own opinions. A good life makes a man wise towards God, and gives him experience in many things.[5] The more humble and obedient to God a man is, the more wise and at peace he will be in all that he does.

5. Ecclus. 34:9.

5
On Reading the Holy Scriptures

In the holy Scriptures, truth is to be looked for rather than fair phrases. All sacred scriptures should be read in the spirit in which they were written. In them, therefore, we should seek food for our souls rather than subtleties of speech, and we should as readily read simple and devout books as those that are lofty and profound. Do not be influenced by the importance of the writer, and whether his learning be great or small, but let the love of pure truth draw you to read. Do not inquire, 'Who said this?'[1] but pay attention to what is said.[2]

Men pass away, but the word of the Lord endures for ever.[3]

God speaks to us in different ways,[4] and is no respecter of persons.[5] But curiosity often hinders us in the reading of the Scriptures, for

1. Seneca, *Epist.* XII. 2. S. Augustine, on Ps.36.
3. Ps. 117:2. 4. Col. 3:25. 5. Ecclus. 6:35; 8:9.

we try to examine and dispute over matters that we should pass over and accept in simplicity. If you desire to profit, read with humility, simplicity, and faith, and have no concern to appear learned. Ask questions freely, and listen in silence to the words of the Saints; hear with patience the parables of the fathers, for they are not told without good cause.

6
On Control of the Desires

Whenever a man desires anything inordinately, at once he becomes restless. A proud and avaricious man is never at rest; but a poor and humble man enjoys the riches of peace. A man who is not yet perfectly dead to self is easily tempted, and is overcome even in small and trifling things. And he who is weak in spirit, and still a prey to the senses and bodily passions, can only with great difficulty free himself from worldly lusts. Therefore he is sad when he does so withdraw himself, and is quickly angered when anyone opposes him. Yet, if he obtains what he desires, his conscience is at once stricken by remorse, because he has yielded to his passion, which in no way helps him in his search for peace. True peace of heart can be found only by resisting the passions, not by yielding to them. There is no peace in the heart of a worldly man, who is entirely given to outward affairs; but only in a fervent, spiritual man.

7
On Avoiding Vain Hope and Conceit

Whoever puts his confidence in men or in any creature is very foolish. Do not be ashamed to be the servant of others for love of Jesus Christ, and to appear poor in this world. Do not trust in yourself, but put your whole confidence in God. Do what you are able, and God will bless your good intention. Do not trust in your own knowledge, nor in the cleverness of any man living, but rather in the grace of God, who aids the humble,[1] and humbles the proud.

Do not boast of your possessions, if you have any, nor of the influence of your friends; but glory in God,[2] who gives all things and desires above all things to give you Himself. Do not be vain about your beauty or strength of body, which a little sickness can mar and disfigure. Take no pleasure in your own ability and cleverness, lest you offend God, who has

1. James 6:6.   2. 2 Cor. 10:17.

Himself bestowed on you all your natural gifts.

Do not esteem yourself better than others, lest you appear worse in the eyes of God, who alone knows the heart of man.[3] Do not be proud of your good deeds, for God does not judge as men; and what delights men often displeases God. If you have any good qualities, remember that others have more; and so remain humble. It does you no harm when you esteem all others better than yourself, but it does you great harm when you esteem yourself above others. True peace dwells only in the heart of the humble: but the heart of the proud is ever full of pride and jealousy.

3. Ps. 94:11; John 2:25.

8

On Guarding against Familiarity

Do not open your heart to everyone,[1] but ask counsel of one who is wise and fears God. Be seldom with young people and strangers. Do not flatter the wealthy, and avoid the society of the great. Associate rather with the humble and simple, the devout, and the virtuous, and converse with them on such things as edify. Avoid undue familiarity with the other sex, but commend all good women to God. Desire to be familiar only with God and His angels, and do not seek the acquaintance of men.

We must live in charity with all men, but familiarity with them is not desirable. It sometimes happens that someone personally unknown to us enjoys a high reputation, but that when we meet him, we are not impressed.

1. Ecclus. 8:19.

Similarly, we sometimes imagine that our company is pleasing, when in reality we offend others by our ill behaviour.

9
On Obedience and Discipline

It is an excellent thing to live under obedience to a superior, and not to be one's own master. It is much safer to obey than to rule. Many live under obedience more of necessity than of love, and such people are often discontented and complaining. They will never attain freedom of mind unless they submit with their whole heart for the love of God. Go where you please, but nowhere will you find rest except in humble obedience under the rule of a superior. Preference for other places and desire for change have unsettled many.

Everyone gladly does whatever he most likes, and likes best those who think as he does; but if God is to dwell among us, we must sometimes yield our own opinion for the sake of peace. Who is so wise that he knows all things? So do not place too much reliance on the rightness of your own views, but be ready to consider the views of others. If your opinion is sound, and you forgo it for the love of God and follow that of another, you will win great merit. I have often heard that it is safer to accept advice than to give it. It may even come about that each of two opinions is good; but to refuse to come to an agreement with others when reason or occasion demand it, is a sign of pride and obstinacy.

On Avoiding Talkativeness

Avoid public gatherings as much as possible, for the discussion of worldly affairs becomes a great hindrance even though it be with the best of intentions, for we are quickly corrupted and ensnared by vanity. Often I wish I had remained silent, and had not been among men. But why is it that we are so ready to chatter and gossip with each other, when we so seldom return to silence without some injury to our conscience? The reason why we are so fond of talking with each other is that we think to find consolation in this manner, and to refresh a heart wearied with many cares. And we prefer to speak and think of those things which we like and desire, or of those which we dislike. Alas, however, all this is often to no purpose, for this outward consolation is no small obstacle to inner and divine consolation.

We must watch and pray,[1] that our time may not be spent fruitlessly. When it is right and proper to speak, speak to edify.[2] Evil habits and neglect of spiritual progress are the main cause of our failure to guard the tongue.[3] But devout conversation on spiritual matters greatly furthers our spiritual progress, especially with those who are heart and soul with us in the service of God.[4]

1. Matt. 26:41. 2. Eph. 4:29. 3. James 3:5.
4. Acts 2:42.

On Peace, and Spiritual Progress

We could enjoy much peace if we did not busy ourselves with what other people say and do, for this is no concern of ours. How can anyone remain long at peace who meddles in other people's affairs; who seeks occasion to gad about, and who makes little or no attempt at recollection? Blessed are the single-hearted,[1] for they shall enjoy much peace.[2]

How were some of the Saints so perfect and contemplative? It is because they strove with all their might to mortify in themselves all worldly desires, and could thus cling to God in their inmost heart, and offer themselves freely and wholly to Him. But we are held too firmly by our passions, and are too much concerned with the passing affairs of the world. We seldom completely master a single fault, and have little

---

1. Matt. 5:8. 2. Ps. 37:11.

zeal for our daily progress; therefore we remain spiritually cold or tepid.

If only we were completely dead to self, and free from inner conflict, we could savour spiritual things, and win experience of heavenly contemplation. But the greatest, and indeed the whole obstacle to our advance is that we are not free from passions and lusts, nor do we strive to follow the perfect way of the Saints. But when we encounter even a little trouble, we are quickly discouraged, and turn to human comfort.

If we strove to stand firm in the struggle like men of valour, we should not fail to experience the help of our Lord from heaven. For He is ever ready to help all who fight, trusting in His grace; He also affords us occasions to fight that we may conquer. If we rely only on the outward observances of religion, our devotion will rapidly wane. But let us lay the axe to the root,[3] that, being cleansed from our passions, we may possess our souls in peace.

3. Matt. 3:10.

If each year we would root out one fault, we should soon become perfect. But, alas, the opposite is often the case, that we were better and purer in the beginning of our conversion than after many years of our profession. Our zeal and virtue should grow daily; but it is now held to be a fine thing if a man retains even a little of his first fervour. If only we would do a little violence to ourselves at first, we would later be enabled to do everything easily and gladly.

It is hard to give up old habits, and harder still to conquer our own wills. But if you cannot overcome in small and easy things, how will you succeed in greater? Resist your evil inclinations in the beginning, and break off evil habits, lest they gradually involve you in greater difficulties. Oh, if you could only know how great a peace for yourself and how great a joy for your fellows your good endeavour would win, you would have greater care for your spiritual progress.

12
On the Uses of Adversity

It is good for us to encounter troubles and adversities from time to time, for trouble often compels a man to search his own heart. It reminds him that he is an exile here, and that he can put his trust in nothing in this world. It is good, too, that we sometimes suffer opposition, and that men think ill of us and misjudge us, even when we do and mean well. Such things are an aid to humility, and preserve us from pride and vainglory. For we more readily turn to God as our inward witness, when men despise us and think no good of us.

A man should therefore place such complete trust in God, that he has no need of comfort from men. When a good man is troubled, tempted, or vexed by evil thoughts, he comes more clearly than ever to realize his need of God, without whom he can do nothing good. Then, as he grieves and laments his lot, he turns to prayer amid his misfortunes. He is weary of life, and longs for death to release him, that he may be dissolved, and be with Christ.[1] It is then that he knows with certainty that there can be no complete security nor perfect peace in his life.

1. Phil. 1:23.

13
On Resisting Temptations

So long as we live in this world, we cannot remain without trial and temptation: as Job says, 'Man's life on earth is a warfare.'[1] We must therefore be on guard against temptations, and watchful in prayer,[2] that the Devil find no means of deceiving us; for he never rests, but prowls around seeking whom he may devour.[3] No one is so perfect and holy that he is never tempted, and we can never be secure from temptation.

Although temptations are so troublesome and grievous, yet they are often profitable to us, for by them we are humbled, cleansed, and instructed. All the Saints endured many trials and temptations,[4] and profited by them; but those who could not resist temptations became

1. Job 7:1.   2. 1 Peter 4:7.   3. 1 Peter 5:8.
4. Acts 14:22.

reprobate, and fell away.[5] There is no Order so holy, nor place so secluded, where there are no troubles and temptations.

No man can be entirely free from temptation so long as he lives; for the source of temptation lies within our own nature, since we are born with an inclination towards evil.[6] When one temptation or trial draws to a close, another takes its place; and we shall always have something to fight, for man has lost the blessing of original happiness. Many try to escape temptations, only to encounter them more fiercely, for no one can win victory by flight alone; it is only by patience and true humility that we can grow stronger than all our foes.

The man who only avoids the outward occasions of evil, but fails to uproot it in himself, will gain little advantage. Indeed, temptations will return upon him the sooner, and he will find himself in a worse state than before. Little by little and by patient endurance[7] you will overcome them by God's help, better than

5. Ecclus. 9:11.   6. James 1:14.   7. Col. 1:11.

by your own violence and importunity. Seek regular advice in temptation, and never deal harshly with those who are tempted, but give them such encouragement as you would value yourself.

The beginning of all evil temptation is an unstable mind and lack of trust in God. Just as a ship without a helm is driven to and fro by the waves, so a careless man, who abandons his proper course, is tempted in countless ways. Fire tempers steel,[8] and temptation the just man. We often do not know what we can bear, but temptation reveals our true nature. We need especially to be on our guard at the very onset of temptation, for then the Enemy may be more easily overcome, if he is not allowed to enter the gates of the mind: he must be repulsed at the threshold, as soon as he knocks. Thus the poet Ovid writes, 'Resist at the beginning; the remedy may come too late.'[9] For first there comes into the mind an evil thought: next, a vivid picture: then delight, and urge to

8. Ecclus. 31:26.   9. Ovid, *Remed.*, 91.

evil, and finally consent. In this way the Enemy gradually gains complete mastery, when he is not resisted at first. And the longer a slothful man delays resistance, the weaker he becomes, and the stronger his enemy grows against him.

Some people undergo their heaviest temptations at the beginning of their conversion; some towards the end of their course; others are greatly troubled all their lives; while there are some whose temptations are but light. This is in accordance with the wisdom and justice of God's ordinance, who weighs the condition and merits of every man, and disposes all things for the salvation of those whom He chooses.

We must not despair, therefore, when we are tempted, but earnestly pray God to grant us His help in every need. For, as Saint Paul says, 'With the temptation, God will provide a way to overcome it, that we may be able to bear it.'[10] So, let us humble ourselves under the hand

10. 1 Cor. 10:13.

of God[11] in every trial and trouble, for He will save and raise up the humble in spirit.[12] In all these trials, our progress is tested; in them great merit may be secured, and our virtue become evident. It is no great matter if we are devout and fervent when we have no troubles; but if we show patience in adversity, we can make great progress in virtue. Some are spared severe temptations, but are overcome in the lesser ones of every day, in order that they may be humble, and learn not to trust in themselves, but to recognize their frailty.

11. Judith 8:17; 1 Pet. 5:6.   12. Luke 1:52.

On Avoiding Rash Judgements

Judge yourself, and beware of passing judgement on others. In judging others, we expend our energy to no purpose; we are often mistaken, and easily sin. But if we judge ourselves, our labour is always to our profit. Our judgement is frequently influenced by our personal feelings, and it is very easy to fail in right judgement when we are inspired by private motives. Were God Himself the sole and constant object of our desire, we should not be so easily distressed when our opinions are contradicted.

Very often some inner impulse or outward circumstance draws us to follow it, while many people are always acting in their own interest, although they are not conscious of it. Such appear to enjoy complete tranquillity of mind so long as events accord with their wishes, but at once become distressed and disconsolate when things fall out otherwise. Similarly, differences of opinions and beliefs only too often give rise to quarrels among friends and neighbours, and even between religious and devout people.

Old habits are hard to break, and no one is easily weaned from his own opinions; but if you rely on your own reasoning and ability rather than on the virtue of submission to Jesus Christ,[1] you will but seldom and slowly attain wisdom. For God wills that we become perfectly obedient to Himself, and that we transcend mere reason on the wings of a burning love for Him.

1. Phil. 3:21.

On Deeds Inspired by Love

No motive, even that of affection for anyone, can justify the doing of evil. But to help someone in need, a good work may sometimes be left, or a better undertaken in its place. For in so doing, the good work is not lost, but changed for what is better. Without love, the outward work is of no value; but whatever is done out of love, be it never so little, is wholly fruitful. For God regards the greatness of the love that prompts a man, rather than the greatness of his achievement.

Whoever loves much, does much. Whoever does a thing well, does much. And he does well, who serves the community before his own interests. Often an apparently loving action really springs from worldly motives; for natural inclination, self-will, hope of reward, and our own self-interest will seldom be entirely absent.

Whoever is moved by true and perfect love

is never self-seeking, but desires only that God's glory may be served in all things. He envies none, for he seeks no pleasure for himself, nor does he act for self-gratification, but desires above all good things to merit the blessing of God. All good he ascribes not to men, but to God, from whom all things proceed as from their source, and in whom all the Saints enjoy perfection and peace. Oh, if only a man had a spark of true love in his heart, he would know for certain that all earthly things are full of vanity.

On Bearing with the Faults of Others

Whatever a man is unable to correct in himself or in others, he should bear patiently until God ordains otherwise. Consider, it is perhaps better thus, for the testing of our patience, without which our merits are of little worth. Whenever such obstacles confront you, pray to God that He may grant you His help, and give you grace to endure them in good heart.[1]

If anyone who has been once or twice warned remains obdurate, do not argue with him, but commit all things to God, that His will may be done, and His Name hallowed in all His servants; for He knows well how to bring good out of evil.[2] Strive to be patient; bear with the faults and frailties of others, for you, too, have many faults which others have to bear. If you cannot mould yourself as you

1. Matt. 6:13.   2. Gen. 50:20.

would wish, how can you expect other people to be entirely to your liking? For we require other people to be perfect, but do not correct our own faults.

We wish to see others severely reprimanded; yet we are unwilling to be corrected ourselves. We wish to restrict the liberty of others, but are not willing to be denied anything ourselves. We wish others to be bound by rules, yet we will not let ourselves be bound. It is amply evident, therefore, that we seldom consider our neighbour in the same light as ourselves. Yet, if all men were perfect, what should we have to bear with in others for Christ's sake?

Now, God has thus ordered things that we may learn to bear one another's burdens;[3] for there is no man without his faults, none without his burden.[4] None is sufficient in himself;[5] none is wise in himself;[6] therefore we must support one another,[7] comfort,[8] help, teach, and

3. Gal. 6:2.   4. Gal. 6:5.   5. 2 Cor. 3:5.
6. Prov. 3:7.   7. Col. 3:13.   8. 1 Thess. 5:11.

advise one another. Times of trouble best discover the true worth of a man; they do not weaken him, but show his true nature.

17

On the Monastic Life

If you wish to live in peace and harmony with others, you must learn to discipline yourself in many ways. It is not easy to live in a Religious Community and remain there without fault,[1] persevering faithfully until death.[2] Blessed is he who has thus lived happily and well to the end. If you wish to achieve stability and grow in grace, remember always that you are an exile and pilgrim on this earth.[3] Be content to be accounted a fool for Christ's sake[4] if you wish to be a Religious.

The habit and tonsure by themselves are of small significance; it is the transformation of one's way of life and the complete mortification of the passions that make a true Religious. He who seeks in this life anything but God alone

1. Phil. 3:6.   2. Rev. 2:10.
3. 1 Pet. 2:11; Heb. 11:13.   4. 1 Cor. 4:10.

and the salvation of his soul will find nothing but trouble and grief.[5] Nor can any remain long at peace who does not strive to be the least[6] and servant of all.[7]

You have come here to serve, not to rule. Remember that you are called to labour and endurance, not to pass your time in idleness and gossip, for in this life men are tried like gold in the furnace.[8] No one can remain here, unless he is ready to humble himself with all his heart for love of God.

5. Ecclus. 1:17; Eccles. 1:18.   6. Luke 22:26.
7. 1 Pet. 2:13.   8. Wisd. 3:6.

On the Examples of the Holy Fathers

Consider the glowing examples of the holy Fathers, in whom shone true religion and perfection; compared with them, we do little or nothing. Alas, how can our life be compared with theirs! The Saints and friends of Christ served Our Lord in hunger and thirst, in cold and nakedness, in toil and weariness: in watching and fasting, in prayer and meditation, in persecutions and insults without number.[1]

How countless and constant were the trials endured by the Apostles, Martyrs, Confessors, Virgins, and all those others who strove to follow in the footsteps of Christ. These all hated their lives in this world, that they might keep them to life eternal.[2] How strict and self-denying was the life of the holy Fathers in the desert! How long and grievous the temptations

1. Heb. 11:38; 1 Cor. 4:11.   2. John 12:25.

they endured! How often they were assaulted by the Devil! How frequent and fervent their prayers to God! How strict their fasts! How great their zeal and ardour for spiritual progress! How valiant the battles they fought to overcome their vices! How pure and upright their intention towards God!

All day long they laboured, and the night they gave to continuous prayer; even as they worked, they never ceased from mental prayer. They spent all their time with profit, every hour seeming short in the service of God. They often forgot even their bodily needs in the great sweetness of contemplation. They renounced all riches, dignities, honours, friends and kindred; they desired to possess nothing in this world. Scarcely would they take the necessities of life, and only with reluctance would they provide for the needs of the body. Thus, though destitute of earthly goods, they were abundantly rich in grace and all virtues. Outwardly they were poor, but inwardly they were refreshed with grace and heavenly consolation. They were strangers to the world, but to God they were dear and familiar friends.[3] To themselves they were nothing, but in the eyes of God they were precious and beloved. Grounded in true humility, they lived in simple obedience, they walked in charity and patience;[4] and thus daily increased in the Spirit, and received great grace from God. They were given for an example to all Religious, and they should encourage us to advance in holiness, rather than the lukewarm should incline us to laxness.

How deep was the fervour of all Religious at the foundation of their Order! How great was their devotion in prayer, and their zeal for virtue! How strict was their observance of the Rule! What respect and obedience to the direction of the Superior flourished in those days! Their examples still witness that they were indeed holy and perfect men, who fought valiantly, and trampled the world under their feet. But in these days, any who is not a breaker of rules, or who obeys with patience is accounted outstanding!

3. Exod. 33:11.   4. Ephes. 5:2.

Oh, the carelessness and coldness of this present time! Sloth and lukewarmness make life wearisome for us, and we soon lose our early fervour! May the longing to grow in grace not remain dormant in you, who have been privileged to witness so many examples of the holy life.

19

On the Practices of a Good Religious

The life of a good Religious should shine with all the virtues, that he may be inwardly as he appears outwardly to men. Indeed, there should rightly be far more inward goodness than appears outwardly, for God Himself searches all hearts. We must revere Him above all things, and live purely in His sight as the angels. Each day we should renew our resolution, and bestir ourselves to fervour, as though it were the first day of our conversion, and say, 'Help me, O Lord God, in my good resolve and in your holy service: grant me this day to begin perfectly, for hitherto I have accomplished nothing.'

As our purpose is, so will our spiritual progress be, and we need to be truly diligent if we wish to progress far. For if a man of firm resolution often encounters failure, how can any who seldom makes any firm resolve achieve anything? We fail in our purposes in various ways, and the light omission of our spiritual exercises seldom passes without certain loss to our souls. The resolution of good men depends more on the grace of God than on their own wisdom, and they put their whole trust in Him in all their undertakings. Man proposes, but God disposes,[1] and man's destiny is not in his own hands.[2]

If any of our proper exercises are omitted in order to perform some act of mercy or help a brother, they may be resumed later. But if they are lightly set aside out of sloth or carelessness, this is blameworthy indeed, and will prove harmful to our souls. Try as we will, we shall still fail all too easily in many things. Nevertheless, we should always have a firm resolve, especially against such faults as most hinder our progress. We should carefully examine and order both our inner and outer life, since both are vital to our advance.

Although we cannot always preserve our

---

1. Prov. 16:9. 2. Jer. 10:23.

recollection, yet we must do so from time to time, and at the least once a day, either in the morning or the evening. In the morning form your intention, and at night examine your conduct, what you have done, said, and thought during the day, for in each of these you may have often offended both God and your neighbour. Arm yourself manfully against the wickedness of the Devil;[3] control the appetite, and you will more easily control all bodily desires. Never be entirely idle, but be reading or writing, in prayer or in meditation, or else be engaged in some work for the common good. But undertake manual employments with discretion, for they are not to be practised by all men alike. Those spiritual exercises which are not obligatory should not be made in public; for whatever is purely personal is best done in private.

Take care not to become careless in the common observances, preferring your personal devotions. But when you have fully and faith-

---

3. Eph. 6:11.

fully fulfilled all that you are bound to do, then, if there be time left, employ it in your own devotions. All cannot use the same kind of spiritual exercises, but one suits this person, and another that. Different devotions are suited also to the Seasons, some being best for the Festivals, and others for ordinary days. We find some helpful in temptations, others in peace and quietness. Some things we like to consider when we are sad, and others when we are full of joy in the Lord.

At the great Festivals good spiritual exercises should be renewed, and the prayers of the Saints implored more fervently than ever. From one Festival to another we should resolve so to live, as though we were then to depart from this world and come to the heavenly Feast. During holy seasons, therefore, we should prepare ourselves with care, and live ever more devoutly, keeping every observance more strictly, as though we were soon to receive the reward of our labours from God Himself.

If this reward be delayed, let us consider that we are not yet ready or worthy of the great glory which will be revealed[4] in us at the appointed time: and let us strive to prepare ourselves better for our departure from this world, 'Blessed is the servant,' writes Luke the Evangelist, 'whom the Lord, when He comes, will find ready. I tell you truly that He will set him over all His possessions.'[5]

4. Rom. 8:18.   5. Matt. 24:47.

20

On the Love of Solitude and Silence

Choose a suitable time for recollection and frequently consider the loving-kindness of God. Do not read to satisfy curiosity or to pass the time, but study such things as move your heart to devotion. If you avoid unnecessary talk and aimless visits, listening to news and gossip, you will find plenty of suitable time to spend in meditation on holy things. The greatest Saints used to avoid the company of men[1] whenever they were able, and chose rather to serve God in solitude.

A wise man once said: 'As often as I have been among men, I have returned home a lesser man.'[2] We often share this experience, when we spend much time in conversation. It is easier to keep silence altogether than not to talk more than we should. It is easier to remain quietly

1. Heb. 9:38. 2. Seneca, *Epist.* VII.

at home than to keep due watch over ourselves in public. Therefore, whoever is resolved to live an inward and spiritual life must, with Jesus, withdraw from the crowd.[3] No man can live in the public eye without risk to his soul, unless he who would prefer to remain obscure. No man can safely speak unless he who would gladly remain silent. No man can safely command, unless he who has learned to obey well. No man can safely rejoice, unless he possesses the testimony of a good conscience.

The security of the Saints was grounded in the fear of God, nor were they less careful and humble because they were resplendent in great virtues and graces. But the security of the wicked springs from pride and presumption, and ends in self-deception. Never promise yourself security in this life, even though you seem to be a good monk or a devout hermit.

Those who stand highest in the esteem of men are most exposed to grievous peril, since they often have too great a confidence in

3. Mark 6:31.

themselves. It is therefore more profitable to many that they should not altogether escape temptations, but be often assailed lest they become too secure and exalted in their pride, or turn too readily to worldly consolations. How good a conscience would he keep if a man never sought after passing pleasures nor became preoccupied with worldly affairs! If only a man could cast aside all useless anxiety and think only on divine and salutary things, how great would be his peace and tranquillity!

No one is worthy of heavenly comfort, unless they have diligently exercised themselves in holy contrition. If you desire heartfelt contrition, enter into your room, and shut out the clamour of the world, as it is written, 'Commune with your own heart, and in your chamber, and be still.'[4] Within your cell you will discover what you will only too often lose abroad. The cell that is dwelt in continually becomes a delight, but ill kept it breeds weariness of spirit. If in the beginning of your

4. Ps. 4:4; Isa. 26:20.

religious life you have dwelt in it and kept it well, it will later become a dear friend and a welcome comfort.

In silence and quietness the devout soul makes progress and learns the hidden mysteries of the Scriptures.[5] There she finds floods of tears in which she may nightly wash and be cleansed.[6] For the further she withdraws from all the tumult of the world, the nearer she draws to her Maker. For God with His holy angels will draw near to him who withdraws himself from his friends and acquaintances. It is better to live in obscurity and to seek the salvation of his soul, than to neglect this even to work miracles. It is commendable in a Religious, therefore, to go abroad but seldom, to avoid being seen, and to have no desire to see men.

Why do you long to see that which is not lawful for you to possess? The world itself passes away, and all the desires of it.[7] The desires of the senses call you to roam abroad,

5. Ecclus. 39:1–3.   6. Ps. 6:6.   7. 1 John 2:17.

but when their hour is spent, what do you bring back but a burdened conscience and a distracted heart? A cheerful going out often brings a sad home-coming, and a merry evening brings a sorry morning. For every bodily pleasure brings joy at first, but at length it bites and destroys.[8]

What can you see elsewhere that you cannot see here?[9] Look at the sky, the earth, and all the elements, for of these all things are made. What can you see anywhere under the sun that can endure for long? You hope, perhaps to find complete satisfaction; but this you will never do. Were you to see all things at present in existence spread out before your eyes, what would it be but an unprofitable vision?[10] Lift up your eyes to God on high,[11] and beg forgiveness for your sin and neglectfulness. Leave empty matters to the empty-headed, and give your attention to those things that God commands you. Shut your door upon you,[12] and

8. Prov. 23: 31, 32. 9. Eccles. 1:10. 10. Eccles. 2:11.
11. Ps. 121:1; Isa. 40:26. 12. Matt. 6:6; Isa. 26:20.

call upon Jesus the Beloved. Remain with Him in your cell, for you will not find so great a peace anywhere else. Had you never gone out and listened to idle talk, you would the better have remained perfectly at peace. But if it pleases you to hear the news of the world, you must always suffer disquiet of heart as a result.

21

On Contrition of Heart

If you wish to grow in holiness, you must live in the fear of God.[1] Do not seek too much freedom, but discipline all your senses, and do not engage in foolish occupations; give yourself rather to contrition of heart, and you will find true devotion. Contrition reveals to us many good things to which dissipation rapidly blinds us. It is a wonder that any man can ever feel perfectly contented with this present life, if he weighs and considers his state of banishment, and the many perils which beset his soul.

Levity of heart and neglect of our faults make us insensible to the proper sorrows of the soul, and we often engage in empty laughter when we should rightly weep. There is no real liberty and true joy, save in the fear of God with a

1. Prov. 1:7; 19:23.

quiet conscience. Happy is he who can set aside every hindering distraction, and recall himself to the single purpose of contrition. Happy is he who abjures whatever may stain or burden his conscience. Fight manfully, for one habit overcomes another. If you are content to let others alone, they will gladly leave you to accomplish your purpose unhindered.

Do not busy yourself with the affairs of others, nor concern yourself with the policies of your superiors. Watch yourself at all times, and correct yourself before you correct your friends.

Do not be grieved if you do not enjoy popular favour; grieve rather that you do not live as well and carefully as befits a servant of God, and a devout religious person. It is often better and safer not to have many comforts in this life, especially those of the body. Yet, if we seldom or never feel God's comfort, the fault is our own; for we neither seek contrition of heart, nor entirely forgo all vain and outward consolations.

Consider yourself unworthy of God's comfort, but rather deserving of much suffering. When a man is perfectly contrite, this present world becomes grievous and bitter to him. A good man always finds cause for grief and tears; for whether he considers himself or his neighbours, he knows that no man lives without trouble in this life. And the more strictly he examines himself, the more cause he finds for sorrow. Our sins and vices are grounds for rightful sorrow and contrition of heart; for they have so strong a hold on us that we are seldom able to contemplate heavenly things.

If you had more concern for a holy death than a long life, you would certainly be zealous to live better. And were you to ponder in your mind on the pains of Hell and Purgatory,[2] you would readily endure toil and sorrow, and would shrink from no kind of hardship. But because considerations of this kind do not move the heart, we remain cold and unresponsive, clinging to old delights.

2. Matt. 25:41.

It is often our lack of spiritual life that allows our wretched body to rebel so easily. Humbly beg Our Lord, therefore, to grant you the spirit of contrition, and say with the Prophet, 'Feed me, O Lord, with the bread of tears, and give me plenteousness of tears to drink.'[3]

3. Ps. 80:5.

22

On Human Misery

Wherever you are and wherever you turn, you will not find happiness until you turn to God. Why are you so distressed when events do not turn out as you wish and hope? Is there anyone who enjoys everything as he wishes? Neither you, nor I, nor anyone else on earth. There is no one in the world without trouble or anxiety, be he King or Pope. Whose, then, is the happiest lot? Surely, he who is able to suffer for love of God.

Many weak and foolish people[1] say, 'See what a good life that man enjoys! He is so rich, so great, so powerful, so distinguished!' But raise your eyes to the riches of Heaven, and you will see that all the riches of this world are as nothing. All are uncertain and even burdensome, for they are never enjoyed without some

---

1. Luke 12:19.

anxiety or fear. The happiness of man does not consist in abundance of this world's goods,[2] for a modest share is sufficient for him. The more spiritual a man desires to become, the more bitter does this present life grow for him, for he sees and realizes more clearly the defects and corruptions of human nature. For to eat and drink, to wake and sleep, to rest and labour, and to be subject to all the necessities of nature is a great trouble and affliction to the devout man, who would rather be released and set free from all sin.[3]

The inner life of man is greatly hindered in this life by the needs of the body. Thus, the Prophet devoutly prays that he may be set free from them, saying, 'Lord, deliver me from my necessities!'[4] Woe to those who refuse to recognize their own wretchedness, and doubly woe to those who love this miserable and corruptible life![5] For some cling so closely to it, that although by working or begging they can

2. Prov. 19:1. 3. Rom. 7:24; 2 Cor. 5:2.
4. Ps. 25:16. 5. Rom. 8:21.

hardly win the bare necessities, they would yet be willing to live here for ever if it were possible, caring nothing for the Kingdom of God.

How crazy and lacking in faith are such people, who are so deeply engrossed in earthly affairs that they care for nothing but material things![6] These unhappy wretches will at length know to their sorrow how vile and worthless were the things that they loved. But the Saints of God and all the devoted friends of Christ paid little heed to bodily pleasures, nor to prosperity in this life, for all their hopes and aims were directed towards those good things that are eternal.[7] Their whole desire raised them upward to things eternal and invisible, so that the love of things visible could not drag them down. My brother, do not lose hope of progress in the spiritual life;[8] you have still time and opportunity.

Why put off your good resolution? Rise and begin this very moment, and say, 'Now is the time to be up and doing; now is the time to

6. Rom. 8:5.   7. 1 Pet. 1:4.   8. Heb. 10:35.

fight; now is the time to amend.'[9] When things go badly and you are in trouble, then is the time to win merit. You must pass through fire and water, before you can come into the place of rest.[10] You will never overcome your vices, unless you discipline yourself severely. For so long as we wear this frail body, we cannot be without sin, nor can we live without weariness and sorrow. We would gladly be free from all troubles; but since we have lost our innocence through sin, we have also lost true happiness. We must therefore have patience,[11] and wait for God's mercy, until this wickedness pass away, and death be swallowed up in life.[12]

How great is the frailty of man, ever prone to evil![13] Today you confess your sins; tomorrow you again commit the very sins you have confessed! Now you resolve to guard against them, and within the hour you act as though you had never made any resolution! Remembering, then, our weakness and instability, it is proper

9. 2 Cor. 6:2. 10. Ps. 66:11. 11. Heb. 10:36.
12. 2 Cor. 5:4. 13. Gen. 6:5.

to humble ourselves, and never to have a high opinion of ourselves. For we can easily lose by carelessness that which by God's grace and our own efforts we had hardly won.

What will become of us in the end if our zeal so quickly grows cold? Unhappy our fate, if we rest on our oars as though we had already reached a haven of peace and security,[14] when in fact no sign of holiness is apparent in our lives. It would be good for us to be instructed once more, like good novices, in the ways of the good life; there would then be some hope of our future improvement and greater spiritual progress.

14. 1 Thess. 5:3.

23

A Meditation on Death

Very soon the end of your life will be at hand:
consider, therefore, the state of your soul.
Today a man is here; tomorrow he is gone.[1]
And when he is out of sight, he is soon out of
mind. Oh, how dull and hard is the heart of
man, which thinks only of the present, and does
not provide against the future! You should
order your every deed and thought, as though
today were the day of your death. Had you a
good conscience, death would hold no terrors
for you;[2] even so, it were better to avoid sin
than to escape death.[3] If you are not ready to
die today, will tomorrow find you better prepared?[4] Tomorrow is uncertain; and how can
you be sure of tomorrow?

Of what use is a long life, if we amend so

1. 1 Macc. 2:63.   2. Luke 12:37.   3. Wisd. 4:16.
4. Matt. 24:44.

little? Alas, a long life often adds to our sins rather than to our virtue!

Would to God that we might spend a single day really well! Many recount the years since their conversion, but their lives show little sign of improvement. If it is dreadful to die, it is perhaps more dangerous to live long. Blessed is the man who keeps the hour of his death always in mind, and daily prepares himself to die. If you have ever seen anyone die, remember that you, too, must travel the same road.[5]

Each morning remember that you may not live until evening; and in the evening, do not presume to promise yourself another day. Be ready at all times,[6] and so live that death may never find you unprepared. Many die suddenly and unexpectedly; for at an hour that we do not know the Son of Man will come.[7] When your last hour strikes, you will begin to think very differently of your past life, and grieve deeply that you have been so careless and remiss.

5. Heb. 9:27.   6. Luke 21:36.   7. Matt. 24:44.

Happy and wise is he who endeavours to be during his life as he wishes to be found at his death. For these things will afford us sure hope of a happy death; perfect contempt of the world; fervent desire to grow in holiness; love of discipline; the practice of penance; ready obedience; self-denial; the bearing of every trial for the love of Christ. While you enjoy health, you can do much good; but when sickness comes, little can be done. Few are made better by sickness, and those who make frequent pilgrimages seldom acquire holiness by so doing.

Do not rely on friends and neighbours, and do not delay the salvation of your soul to some future date, for men will forget you sooner than you think. It is better to make timely provision and to acquire merit in this life, than to depend on the help of others. And if you have no care for your own soul, who will have care for you in time to come? The present time is most precious; now is the accepted time, now is the day of salvation.[8] It is sad that you do not employ

8. 2 Cor. 6:2.

your time better, when you may win eternal life hereafter. The time will come when you will long for one day or one hour in which to amend; and who knows whether it will be granted?

Dear soul, from what peril and fear you could free yourself, if you lived in holy fear, mindful of your death. Apply yourself so to live now, that at the hour of death, you may be glad and unafraid. Learn now to die to the world, that you may begin to live with Christ.[9] Learn now to despise all earthly things, that you may go freely to Christ. Discipline your body now by penance, that you may enjoy a sure hope of salvation.

Foolish man, how can you promise yourself a long life, when you are not certain of a single day?[10] How many have deceived themselves in this way, and been snatched unexpectedly from life! You have often heard how this man was slain by the sword; another drowned; how another fell from a high place and broke his

9. Rom. 6:8.   10. Luke 12:20.

neck; how another died at table; how another met his end in play. One perishes by fire, another by the sword, another from disease, another at the hands of robbers. Death is the end of all men;[11] and the life of man passes away suddenly as a shadow.[12]

Who will remember you when you are dead? Who will pray for you? Act now, dear soul; do all you can; for you know neither the hour of your death, nor your state after death. While you have time, gather the riches of everlasting life.[13] Think only of your salvation, and care only for the things of God. Make friends now, by honouring the Saints of God and by following their example, that when this life is over, they may welcome you to your eternal home.[14]

Keep yourself a stranger and pilgrim upon earth,[15] to whom the affairs of this world are of no concern. Keep your heart free and lifted

---

11. Eccles. 7:2.   12. Ps. 34:7; 144:4.
13. Luke 12:33; Gal. 6:8.   14. Luke 16:9.
15. I Pet. 2:11.

up to God, for here you have no abiding city.[16] Daily direct your prayers and longings to Heaven, that at your death your soul may merit to pass joyfully into the presence of God.

16. Heb. 13:14.

24

On Judgement, and the
Punishment of Sinners

Always keep in mind your last end, and how you will stand before the just Judge[1] from whom nothing is hid, who cannot be influenced by bribes and excuses, and who judges with justice.[2] O wretched and foolish sinner, who tremble before the anger of man, how will you answer to God,[3] who knows all your wickedness? Why do you not prepare yourself against the Day of Judgement, when no advocate can defend or excuse you, but each man will be hard put to answer for himself? While you live, your labour is profitable and your tears acceptable, for sorrow both cleanses the soul and makes peace with God.

The patient man undergoes a great and wholesome purgation; while suffering injuries,

1. Heb. 10:31.   2. Isa. 11:4.   3. Job 31:14.

he grieves yet more for the malice of others than for his own wrongs; he gladly prays for his enemies, and from his heart forgives their offences; he does not hesitate to ask pardon of others; he is more easily moved to compassion than to anger; he rules himself with strictness, and endeavours to make the body subject to the spirit in all things. It is better to expiate our sins and overcome our vices now, than to reserve them for purgation hereafter; but we deceive ourselves by our inordinate love of the body.

What will the flames feed upon, but your sins? The more you spare yourself now, and indulge the desires of the body, the more severe will be your punishment hereafter, and the more fuel you gather for the flames. In whatever things a man sins, in those will he be the more severely punished.[4] Then will the slothful be spurred by fiery goads, and the gluttonous tormented by dire hunger and thirst. Then will the luxurious and pleasure-loving be plunged

4. Wisd. 11:17.

into burning pitch and stinking sulphur, while the envious will howl their grief like wild dogs.

There is no vice that will not receive its proper retribution. The proud will be subjected to the deepest humiliation, and the greedy experience misery and want. One hour's punishment then will be more bitter than a century of penance on earth. There will be neither rest nor comfort for the damned; but here we sometimes enjoy rest from our toil, and enjoy the comfort of our friends. Therefore, live rightly now, and grieve for your sins, that in the Day of Judgement you may stand secure in the company of the Blessed. For then shall the righteous stand with great boldness before those who have afflicted and oppressed them.[5] Then will he who now submits humbly to the judgement of man stand to judge others. Then will the poor and humble have great confidence, while the proud are encompassed by fears on every side.

It will then be seen that he who learned to

5. Wisd. 5:1.

be counted a fool and despised for Christ's sake in this world was indeed wise.[6] Then will he be glad for every trial patiently borne, and the mouth of the wicked will be sealed.[7] Then will every devout man be glad and the ungodly grieve. Then will he who kept his body in subjection[8] have greater joy than he who lavished every pleasure upon it. Then will the rags of the poor shine with splendour, and the gorgeous raiment become tarnished. Then will the humble cottage of the poor be preferred to the gilded palace. Then will steadfast patience be of more avail than all worldly power. Then will humble obedience be exalted above all worldly cunning. Then will a good and clean conscience bring more joy than learned philosophy. Then will contempt for riches far outweigh all the treasures of the world. Then will devout prayer yield greater pleasure than fine fare. Then will you rejoice more in having kept silence than in much talking. Then will holy deeds count for more than fine words. Then will a disciplined

6. 1 Cor. 4:10.   7. Ps. 107:42.   8. 1 Cor. 9:27.

life and hard penance prove of more worth than all worldly delights.

Learn to endure a little now, that you may spare yourself more grievous troubles. Prove here what you can endure hereafter. If you can endure so little now, how could you endure the pains of hell? Be assured that a man cannot enjoy both kinds of happiness; he cannot enjoy all the pleasures of this life, and also reign with Christ in Heaven. Moreover, if up to this very day you had lived in enjoyment of all honours and pleasures, how would all these profit you if you were to die at this moment? All, therefore, is vanity, save to love God and serve Him alone. For he who loves God with all his heart fears neither death, punishment, judgement, nor hell; for perfect love enjoys sure access to God.[9] But he who continues to delight in wickedness, what wonder is it if he fears death and judgement? Nevertheless, it is good that, if the love of God does not restrain you from sin, the fear of hell at least should restrain you. For he

9. Rom. 8:39.

who sets aside the fear of God cannot long continue in a good life, but will rapidly fall into the snares of the Devil.

25

On the Zealous Amendment of Our Life

Be watchful[1] and diligent in the service of God, and frequently consider why you are come here, and why you have renounced the world. Was it not that you might live to God, and become a spiritual man? Endeavour, then, to make progress, and you will soon receive the reward of your labours; then neither fear nor sorrow will be able to trouble you. Labour for a short while now, and you will find great peace of soul, and everlasting joy. If you remain faithful in all your doings, be sure that God will be faithful and generous in rewarding you.[2] Keep a firm hope that you will win the victor's crown; but do not be over confident, lest you become indolent and self-satisfied.

There was once a man who was very anxious, and wavered between fear and hope. One

1. 2 Tim. 4:5.   2. Ecclus. 51:30.

day, overcome with sadness, he lay prostrate in prayer before the altar in church, and pondering these matters in his mind, said, 'Oh, if only I knew that I should always persevere!' Then he heard within his heart an answer from God: 'If you knew this, what would you do? Do now what you would then, and all will be well.' So, comforted and strengthened, he committed himself to the will of God, and his anxious uncertainty vanished. Nor did he wish any longer to inquire into what would happen to him, but strove the more earnestly to learn the perfect and acceptable will of God,[3] whenever he began or undertook any good work.[4]

'Hope in the Lord, and do good,' says the Prophet: 'dwell in the land, and you shall be fed with its riches.'[5] There is one thing that deters many in their spiritual progress and zeal for amendment, namely, fear of the difficulties and the cost of victory. But rest assured that those who grow in virtue beyond their fellows

---

3. Rom. 12:2.   4. 2 Tim. 3:17.   5. Ps. 37:3.

are they who fight most manfully to overcome whatever is most difficult and distasteful to them. For the more completely a man overcomes and cleanses himself in spirit, the more he profits and deserves abundant grace.

All men do not have the same things to overcome and mortify. But whoever is diligent and zealous – even though he has stronger passions to subdue – will certainly make greater progress than another, who is naturally self-controlled, but less zealous for holiness. Two things in particular are a great help to amendment of life – a forcible withdrawal from any vice to which our nature inclines, and a fervent pursuit of any grace of which we stand in particular need. Especially study to avoid and overcome those things that most displease you in other people.

Strive to progress in all things, and let any examples that you see or hear inspire you to imitate them. But if you observe anything blameworthy, take care not to do the same yourself. And should you ever have done so, amend your conduct without delay. As you observe others, so do others observe you.[6] How glad and pleasant it is to see fervent and devout brethren observing good manners and good discipline.[7] And how sad and painful to see any who are disorderly and fail to live up to their calling. How harmful it is, if they neglect the true purpose of their vocation, and turn to matters that are not their proper concern.

Remember your avowed purpose, and keep ever before you the likeness of Christ crucified. As you meditate on the life of Jesus Christ, you should grieve that you have not tried more earnestly to conform yourself to Him, although you have been a long while in the way of God. A Religious who earnestly and devoutly contemplates the most holy Life and Passion of Our Lord will find in it an abundance of all things profitable and needful to him, nor need he seek any other model than Jesus. Oh, if Jesus Crucified would come into our hearts, how quickly and fully we should be instructed!

A zealous Religious readily accepts and

6. Matt. 7:3.   7. Eph. 5:2.

obeys all commands. But a careless and luke-warm Religious has trouble after trouble, and finds sorrow on every side because he lacks true inward consolation, and is forbidden to seek it outside. Therefore a Religious who disregards his Rule exposes himself to dreadful ruin. And he who desires an easier and undisciplined life will always be unstable, for one thing or another will always displease him.

Observe how many behave, who live strictly under the monastic discipline. They seldom go out, they live retired, they eat the poorest food; they work hard, they talk little, they keep long watches; they rise early, they spend much time in prayer, they study much, and always guard themselves with discipline. Consider the Carthusians, the Cistercians, and the monks and nuns of the various Orders, how they rise each night to sing praises to Our Lord. Were you slothful, this should shame you, when so great a company of Religious are beginning the praises of God.

Would that our sole occupation were the per-petual praise of the Lord our God with heart and voice! Had you no need of food, drink or rest, you could praise God without ceasing, and give yourself wholly to spiritual things. You would be far happier than now, when you are compelled to serve the needs of the body. Would that these needs did not exist, so that we might enjoy the spiritual feasts of the soul, which, alas, we taste so seldom.

When a man no longer seeks his comfort from any creature, then he first begins to enjoy God perfectly, and he will be well content with whatever befalls him. Then he will neither rejoice over having much, nor grieve over having little, but will commit himself fully and trustfully to God, who is All[8] in all to him: in Him nothing perishes or dies, for all things live for Him, and serve His will continually.

Always remember your end,[9] and that lost time never returns. Without care and diligence, you will never acquire virtue. If you begin to grow careless, all will begin to go amiss with you. But if you give yourself to prayer, you will

8. Col. 3:11.   9. Ecclus. 7:36.

find great peace, and your toil will grow lighter by the help of God's grace and your love of virtue. The fervent and sincere man is prepared for anything. The war against our vices and passions is harder than any physical toil; and whoever fails to overcome his lesser faults will gradually fall into greater.[10] Your evenings will always be tranquil if you have spent the day well. Watch yourself, bestir yourself, admonish yourself; and whatever others may do, never neglect your own soul. The stricter you are with yourself, the greater is your spiritual progress.

10. Ecclus. 19:1.

PENGUIN 60s CLASSICS

PENGUIN 60s CLASSICS

HENRY JAMES · *The Lesson of the Master*
FRANZ KAFKA · *The Judgement*
THOMAS À KEMPIS · *Counsels on the Spiritual Life*
HEINRICH VON KLEIST · *The Marquise of O—*
LIVY · *Hannibal's Crossing of the Alps*
NICCOLÒ MACHIAVELLI · *The Art of War*
SIR THOMAS MALORY · *The Death of King Arthur*
GUY DE MAUPASSANT · *Boule de Suif*
FRIEDRICH NIETZSCHE · *Zarathustra's Discourses*
OVID · *Orpheus in the Underworld*
PLATO · *Phaedrus*
EDGAR ALLAN POE · *The Murders in the Rue Morgue*
ARTHUR RIMBAUD · *A Season in Hell*
JEAN-JACQUES ROUSSEAU · *Meditations of a Solitary Walker*
ROBERT LOUIS STEVENSON · *Dr Jekyll and Mr Hyde*
TACITUS · *Nero and the Burning of Rome*
HENRY DAVID THOREAU · *Civil Disobedience*
LEO TOLSTOY · *The Death of Ivan Ilyich*
IVAN TURGENEV · *Three Sketches from a Hunter's Album*
MARK TWAIN · *The Man That Corrupted Hadleyburg*
GIORGIO VASARI · *Lives of Three Renaissance Artists*
EDITH WHARTON · *Souls Belated*
WALT WHITMAN · *Song of Myself*
OSCAR WILDE · *The Portrait of Mr W. H.*

ANONYMOUS WORKS

Beowulf and Grendel   *Buddha's Teachings*
Gilgamesh and Enkidu   *Krishna's Dialogue on the Soul*
Tales of Cú Chulaind   *Two Viking Romances*

READ MORE IN PENGUIN

For complete information about books available from Penguin and how to order them, please write to us at the appropriate address below. Please note that for copyright reasons the selection of books varies from country to country.

IN THE UNITED KINGDOM: Please write to *Dept. EP, Penguin Books Ltd, Bath Road, Harmondsworth, Middlesex UB7 0DA*.

IN THE UNITED STATES: Please write to *Consumer Sales, Penguin USA, P.O. Box 999, Dept. 17109, Bergenfield, New Jersey 07621-0120*. VISA and MasterCard holders call 1-800-253-6476 to order Penguin titles.

IN CANADA: Please write to *Penguin Books Canada Ltd, 10 Alcorn Avenue, Suite 300, Toronto, Ontario M4V 3B2*.

IN AUSTRALIA: Please write to *Penguin Books Australia Ltd, P.O. Box 257, Ringwood, Victoria 3134*.

IN NEW ZEALAND: Please write to *Penguin Books (NZ) Ltd, Private Bag 102902, North Shore Mail Centre, Auckland 10*.

IN INDIA: Please write to *Penguin Books India Pvt Ltd, 706 Eros Apartments, 56 Nehru Place, New Delhi 110 019*.

IN THE NETHERLANDS: Please write to *Penguin Books Netherlands bv, Postbus 3507, NL-1001 AH Amsterdam*.

IN GERMANY: Please write to *Penguin Books Deutschland GmbH, Metzlerstrasse 26, 60594 Frankfurt am Main*.

IN SPAIN: Please write to *Penguin Books S. A., Bravo Murillo 19, 1º B, 28015 Madrid*.

IN ITALY: Please write to *Penguin Italia s.r.l., Via Felice Casati 20, I-20124 Milano*.

IN FRANCE: Please write to *Penguin France S. A., 17 rue Lejeune, F-31000 Toulouse*.

IN JAPAN: Please write to *Penguin Books Japan, Ishikiribashi Building, 2-5-4, Suido, Bunkyo-ku, Tokyo 112*.

IN GREECE: Please write to *Penguin Hellas Ltd, Dimocritou 3, GR-106 71 Athens*.

IN SOUTH AFRICA: Please write to *Longman Penguin Southern Africa (Pty) Ltd, Private Bag X08, Bertsham 2013*.